中国天然气发展报告

（2016）

国家能源局石油天然气司

国务院发展研究中心资源与环境政策研究所

国土资源部油气资源战略研究中心

石油工业出版社

China Natural Gas Development Report

(2016)

Oil and Gas Department, National Energy Administration

Institute for Resources and Environmental Policies, Development Research Center of the State Council

Center for Oil and Gas Resource Strategies, Ministry of Land and Resources

Petroleum Industry Press

《中国天然气发展报告(2016)》编委会

(以下按姓氏笔画排序)

主　　任：
　　王一鸣　李凡荣　汪　民
副 主 任：
　　刘德顺　高世楫　谢承祥
委　　员：
　　王　晶　白彦锋　刘　冰　陆　丰
　　李英华　吴裕根　赵昌文　洪　涛
　　郭焦锋　韩景宽　蔡圣华　潘继平
顾　　问：
　　马永生　张玉清　金之钧　赵文智
　　郝　芳　康玉柱　童晓光　曾兴球
总协调人：
　　郭焦锋
编写单位：
　　国家能源局石油天然气司
　　国务院发展研究中心资源与环境政策研究所
　　国土资源部油气资源战略研究中心
支持单位：
　　中国科学院科技战略咨询研究院
　　中国能源研究会
　　中国石油和化学工业联合会
　　上海国际能源交易中心
　　中国石油规划总院
出版和翻译单位：
　　石油工业出版社

China Natural Gas Development Report (2016) Editorial Board

(Following the surname stroke order)

Chairpersons:
　　WANG Yiming　　LI Fanrong　　WANG Min

Deputy Chairpersons:
　　LIU Deshun　　GAO Shiji　　XIE Chengxiang

Committee Members:
　　WANG Jing　　BAI Yanfeng　　LIU Bing　　LU Feng
　　LI Yinghua　　WU Yugen　　ZHAO Changwen　　HONG Tao
　　GUO Jiaofeng　　HAN Jingkuan　　CAI Shenghua　　PAN Jiping

Advisors:
　　MA Yongsheng　　ZHANG Yuqing　　JIN Zhijun　　ZHAO Wenzhi
　　HAO Fang　　KANG Yuzhu　　TONG Xiaoguang　　ZENG Xingqiu

Coordinator:
　　GUO Jiaofeng

Principal Institutions:
　　Oil and Gas Department, National Energy Administration
　　Institute for Resources and Environmental Policies, Development Research
　　　　Center of the State Council
　　Center for Oil and Gas Resource Strategies, Ministry of Land and Resources

Supporting Institutions:
　　Institute of Policy and Management, Chinese Academy of Sciences
　　China Energy Research Society
　　China Petroleum and Chemical Industry Association
　　Shanghai International Energy Exchange Corporation
　　China Petroleum Planning and Engineering Institute

Publishing and Translation:
　　Petroleum Industry Press

前　言

能源是人类生存和发展的重要物质基础，人类文明的进步离不开优质能源的出现和先进能源技术的使用。18世纪英国工业革命之前，柴薪、木炭等生物质是人类的主要能源来源；其后煤炭大规模使用，至19世纪中后期取代生物质成为主要能源；进入20世纪中期以来，石油大量使用，使人类衣、食、住、行发生巨大变化，并定义了"现代社会"形态。煤炭和石油消费为世界带来工业文明巨大进步的同时，也带来了日益严峻的大气环境影响。大气污染防治的根本出路是能源的绿色发展和实施清洁能源替代。天然气是低碳、清洁能源，资源丰富，发达国家大都把天然气作为能源清洁替代的重要选项。美国"页岩革命"大幅度提高了世界对天然气资源储量的预期，天然气已成为世界最具发展潜力的主体能源。

习近平总书记提出"四个革命、一个合作"的发展战略，为中国能源革命指明了方向，是中国发展天然气、推进天然气领域改革遵循的基本原则。2016年在杭州召开的G20峰会上，中国政府签署了《巴黎协定》，承诺在2030年左右实现碳排放达到峰值。走绿色、清洁、低碳的能源发展道路不仅是中国经济社会可持续发展的有力保障，也是中国作为最大发展中国家对全世界庄严承诺的践行，大规模发展天然气势在必行。

Preface

Energy is an essential material for human survival and development. The progress of human civilization cannot be separated from the emergence of high quality energy and the use of advanced energy technologies. Before the British Industrial Revolution in the 18th century, wood, charcoal and other biomass were the main source of energy for mankind. After that coal was used on a large scale, exceeding biomass as the main energy source at the mid- and late 19th century. Since the mid-20th century, the extensive use of oil has resulted in dramatic changes in the life of human, and defined the form of "modern society". While the consumption of coal and oil has brought great progress of industrial civilization to the world, however at the same time, increasingly serious atmospheric environmental impacts have been brought. The fundamental ways to prevent and control air pollution are the greening of energy and the implementation of clean energy replacement. Natural gas is a low-carbon and clean energy with abundant resource. Most developed countries consider natural gas as an important alternative towards a cleaner energy structure. The "Shale Gas Revolution" in the United States has greatly increased the world's estimation of natural gas reserves. Natural gas has become the world's most promising form of energy.

General Secretary Xi Jinping put forward the development strategy of "Four-Revolution, One-Cooperation", pointing out the direction of China's energy revolution and forming the basic principles for China to develop natural gas and to promote the natural gas reform. At the 2016 G20 Summit in Hangzhou, the Chinese Government signed the "Paris Agreement" and promised to achieve carbon emissions peak around by 2030. The green, clean, low carbon energy development path is not only a powerful guarantee for China's sustainable economic and societal development, but also China's practice for its solemn commitment to the world as the largest developing country. Therefore, large-scale development of natural gas is imperative.

目前中国正处于能源转型的关键时期，新能源、新业态不断出现，又值国际油价低位运行，必须抓住这一重要时间窗口，加速推进中国天然气大发展。发布《中国天然气发展报告》，旨在梳理中国天然气的发展现状，明确未来天然气发展定位、方向和目标，阐明天然气发展战略与政策取向，为中国天然气快速发展汇集多方力量，凝聚广泛共识。

Currently, China is in a critical stage of energy transformation with the global feature of new energy and new industries keeping emerging, and international oil price running at a historically low level. It is important to seize the time window to accelerate the development of China's natural gas industry. "China Natural Gas Development Report" is published in order to summarize the development status of natural gas, explain the position, direction and target of natural gas development of China, clarify the strategy and policy orientation, and bring together all the stakeholders as well as reach a broad consensus for the rapid development of China's natural gas industry.

目 录

一、世界天然气发展现状……………………………………1

二、中国天然气发展现状……………………………………7

三、中国天然气发展前景……………………………………17

四、中国天然气战略地位、发展路径和政策取向……………29

结束语…………………………………………………………43

CONTENTS

1. Global Natural Gas Development Status 2

2. China's Natural Gas Development Status 8

3. China's Natural Gas Development Prospects 18

4. China's Natural Gas Development: Strategic Positioning, Growth Pathway and Policy Orientation..................... 30

Concluding Remarks 44

一、世界天然气发展现状[1]

世界天然气资源丰富，供应相对充裕。亚太和中东地区消费量增长迅速、占比逐年提高，亚太地区在世界天然气市场的地位逐渐增强。

（一）世界天然气资源丰富

截至 2014 年底，世界常规天然气可采资源量为 559.5 万亿立方米，累计产量 103.5 万亿立方米；非常规天然气可采资源量为 543.5 万亿立方米（其中致密气 83.6 万亿立方米，页岩气 196.8 万亿立方米，煤层气 52.4 万亿立方米，天然气水合物 184 万亿立方米，其他为水溶气），累计产量 5.9 万亿立方米。按照目前年产量 3.6 万亿立方米测算，世界天然气资源可供开采 200 年以上。

（二）世界天然气产量逐年增加

2005 年世界天然气产量为 2.8 万亿立方米，2015 年增至 3.6 万亿立方米，其中年产量居前五位的国家分别是美国（7673 亿立方米）、俄罗斯（5733 亿立方米）、伊朗（1925 亿立方米）、卡塔尔（1814 亿立方米）和加拿大（1635 亿立方米）。分区域看，2015 年，北美地区产量 9840 亿立方米，占世界总产量的 27.3%；前苏联地区产量 7513.8 亿立方米，占比 20.9%；中东地区产量 6179.0 亿立方米，占比 17.2%；亚太地区产量 5566.6 亿立方米，占比 15.5%。

---

[1] 本节储量、产量、消费量和贸易量统计数据主要来源于《BP 世界能源统计》。

1. Global Natural Gas Development Status[1]

The global natural gas resources are abundant, providing relatively ample supply. The natural gas consumption in Asia-Pacific and Middle East regions has been growing rapidly, with yearly growing proportion of the world total. Asia-Pacific is playing a gradually increasing role in the global natural gas market.

(1) Abundant Global Natural Gas Resources

As of the end of 2014, the global conventional natural gas reserves were 559 Tcm with 103.5 Tcm cumulative production; unconventional gas reserves were 543.5 Tcm (including 83.6 Tcm of tight gas, 196.8 Tcm of shale gas, 52.4 Tcm of coalbed methane, and 184 Tcm of gas hydrate, with the others being water-soluble gas) with 5.9 Tcm cumulative production. Based on the current 3.6 Tcm annual production volume, the global natural gas reserves can last for more than 200 years.

(2) Yearly Increasing of Global Natural Gas Production

The global natural gas production was 2.8 Tcm in 2005 and increased to 3.6 Tcm in 2015, of those production the top five countries were United States (767.3 Bcm), Russia (573.3 Bcm), Iran (192.5 Bcm), Qatar (181.4 Bcm) and Canada (163.5 Bcm), respectively. In terms of regions, in 2015, North America produced 984 Bcm; former Soviet Union produced 751.38 Bcm; Middle East produced 617.9 Bcm; Asia-Pacific produced 556.66 Bcm, accounting for 27.3%, 20.9%, 17.2% and 15.5% of the global total production, respectively.

---

[1] The reserves, production, consumption and trade volume data in this chapter are mainly from "BP Statistical Review of World Energy".

（三）世界天然气消费量持续增长

2005年世界天然气消费量为2.77万亿立方米，2015年增至3.47万亿立方米。2015年天然气在世界一次能源消费中占比为23.7%。2015年天然气消费量超过1000亿立方米的国家有美国（7779.7亿立方米）、俄罗斯（3914.8亿立方米）、中国（1931亿立方米）、伊朗（1912亿立方米）、日本（1134亿立方米）、沙特阿拉伯（1064亿立方米）和加拿大（1025亿立方米）。分区域看，2015年，北美地区占比27.8%，亚太地区占比20.2%，前苏联地区占比16.7%，欧洲地区占比13.3%，中东地区占比14.1%，其中亚太、中东地区天然气消费量快速增长，占比逐年提高，北美、前苏联地区的增速相对较缓，占比呈下降趋势。

（四）世界天然气贸易市场加快发展

世界天然气贸易量占消费量的比重呈增长态势。2005年世界天然气贸易量为7214亿立方米，2015年贸易量增至10424亿立方米，其中管道天然气贸易量7041亿立方米、LNG贸易量3383亿立方米，管道天然气仍是天然气贸易的主要形式。世界天然气贸易流向继续向亚太地区转移。2010-2015年期间，欧洲地区的贸易量共减少384.8亿立方米；而同期亚太地区贸易量共增加886.8亿立方米；北美地区进口管道气和LNG贸易呈平稳下降态势。2015年，世界天然气供需总体宽松，价格大幅下滑。从区域价格看，美国亨利中心的年均价格为2.62美元／百万英热单位,同比跌幅近40%；英国国家平衡点(NBP)年均价格为6.62美元／百万英热单位，同比下跌14%；与"日本一揽子进口原油价格"（JCC）挂钩的亚洲液化天然气（LNG）进口年均价格为10.64美元／百万英热单位，同比下降34.4%。

(3) Continued Growing of Global Natural Gas Consumption

The global natural gas consumption was 2.77 Tcm in 2005 and increased to 3.47 Tcm in 2015. Its proportion in the global primary energy consumption was 23.7% in 2015. Countries with more than 100 Bcm natural gas consumption in 2015 included United States (777.97 Bcm), Russia (391.48 Bcm), China (193.1 Bcm), Iran (191.2 Bcm), Japan (113.4 Bcm), Saudi Arabia (106.4 Bcm) and Canada (102.5 Bcm). In terms of regions, in 2015, North America accounted for 27.8%, Asia-Pacific accounted for 20.2%, former Soviet Union accounted for 16.7%, Europe accounted for 13.3%, and Middle East accounted for 14.1%, of the global total consumption, respectively. Asia-Pacific and Middle East regions have rapid growth in natural gas consumption, with gradually increasing proportion, while the growth rate in North America and former Soviet Union was relatively slow, with decreased proportion.

(4) Accelerated Development of Global Natural Gas Trade Marking

The proportion of the global natural gas consumption trade volume is showing an increasing trend. The global natural gas trade volume was 721.4 Bcm in 2015 and increased to 1042.4 Bcm in 2015, of which pipeline trade volume was 704.1 Bcm and LNG trading volume was 338.3 Bcm, indicating pipeline gas was still the main natural gas trade form. The global natural gas trade continues to shift to Asia-Pacific Region. From 2010 to 2015, Europe's trade volume decreased by 38.48 Bcm, while over the same period Asia-Pacific trade volume increased by 88.68 Bcm; North America's pipeline gas import and LNG trade showed a steady downward trend. In 2015 the global total natural gas supply and demand were generally easing, causing prices to fall sharply. In terms of the regional prices, the annual average price of the Henry Center was $2.62/MMBTU, a nearly 40% year-on-year decline; the British NBP average price was $6.62/MMBTU with a 14% year-on-year decrease; and the Asian LNG average import price linked to "Japan Customs-cleared Crude" (JCC) was $10.64/MMBTU, a 34.4% year-on-year reduction.

（五）世界典型国家天然气发展经验借鉴

世界典型国家天然气发展遵循启动期、发展期、成熟期的产业发展规律，快速发展期一般经历 30 年左右。如美国，1945 年天然气消费量突破 1000 亿立方米，1970 年增至 6000 亿立方米，经历了 25 年的快速发展，期间消费量年均增长约 200 亿立方米；英国 1970 年天然气消费量突破 100 亿立方米，2000 年增至 968 亿立方米，经历了 30 年的快速发展，期间消费量年均增长约 30 亿立方米；日本 1976 年天然气消费量达到 100 亿立方米，2012 年增至 1135 亿立方米，经历了 36 年的快速发展，期间消费量年均增长约 30 亿立方米。

驱动天然气快速发展的因素主要包括政策、资源、基础设施、价格等方面。通常在能源转型中，加大天然气利用由环保问题触发，政策特别是环保政策和产业政策在天然气发展的关键节点起到主要推动作用，而市场化进程则是天然气产业可持续发展的重要保障。19 世纪末 20 世纪初，美国煤炭消费量占一次能源比例达到 80%，1943 年洛杉矶光化学烟雾事件后陆续发布《清洁空气法》《清洁电力计划》等，"页岩革命"进一步加速了"气代煤"进程，到 2015 年，天然气占美国一次能源消费比例升至 29%，煤炭下降为 16%。1952 年伦敦烟雾事件，英国出台《清洁空气法》，伦敦市区及近郊区设禁煤区，1974 年颁布《污染控制法》，严格限制煤炭大气污染物排放，鼓励利用天然气，随着煤炭逐步被天然气和石油所替代，困扰欧洲国家多年的煤烟型污染才得以解决。

(5) Typical Countries' Natural Gas Development Experience

The development of natural gas in typical countries follows the start-up, development and maturation periods, with the rapid development period of about 30 years. The United States, for instance, the natural gas consumption exceeded 100 Bcm in 1945 and increased to 600 Bcm in 1970, after 25 years of rapid development with an average annual consumption growth of about 20 Bcm. UK's natural gas consumption exceeded 10 Bcm in 1970 and increased to 96.8 Bcm in 2000, after 30 years of rapid development with an average 3 Bcm annual consumption growth. Japan's natural gas consumption reached 10 Bcm in 1976 and increased to 113.5 Bcm in 2012, after 36 years of rapid development with an average annual consumption growth of 3 Bcm.

The factors driving the rapid development of natural gas mainly include policy, resource, infrastructure, and price, etc. Usually in energy transformation, the increase of natural gas utilization is triggered by the environmental protection issues. The environmental protection policy and industrial policy particularly have a major role in promoting the development of natural gas in the key stages, while marketization process is an important guarantee for the sustainable development of natural gas industry. At late 19th century and early 20th century, the proportion of coal consumption in primary energy reached 80%. The "Clean Air Act" and "Clean Power Plan" were released after the 1943 Los Angeles Photochemical Smog Event. The "Shale Gas Revolution" further accelerated the United States' "Coal-to-Gas" process and the proportion of natural gas in its primary energy consumption rose to 29% in 2015, while coal decreased to 16%. After the 1952 London Smog Event, UK introduced the "Clean Air Act", setting London and its suburban area as no-coal zone. In 1974 UK issued the "Pollution Control Law", which strictly limited the emissions of air pollutants from coal-burning and encouraged the use of natural gas. With coal being gradually replaced by natural gas and oil, the coal-burning pollution that has plagued European countries for many years was resolved.

二、中国天然气发展现状

中国天然气资源丰富，初步形成多品种、多渠道的多元化供应和"西气东输、北气南下、海气登陆、就近供应"的供气格局。稳定的供应和初具规模的基础设施有力支撑了中国天然气的快速发展，天然气消费市场已遍及中国内地31个省份（自治区、直辖市）。同时，天然气市场化改革有序推进，试点改革探索取得阶段性突破。这些为未来天然气成为中国主体能源打下了良好基础。

（一）中国天然气资源潜力大

全国常规天然气地质资源量90万亿立方米，可采资源量50万亿立方米。埋深4500米以浅页岩气地质资源量122万亿立方米，可采资源量22万亿立方米，具有现实可开发价值的有利区可采资源量5.5万亿立方米。全国埋深2000米以浅煤层气地质资源量30万亿立方米，可采资源量12.5万亿立方米，具有现实可开发价值的有利区可采资源量4万亿立方米。

截至2015年底，全国累计探明常规天然气地质储量13.01万亿立方米，剩余可采储量5.2万亿立方米；累计探明煤层气地质储量6293亿立方米，剩余可采储量3063亿立方米；累计探明页岩气地质储量5441亿立方米，剩余可采储量1302亿立方米。

（二）中国天然气供应能力快速增长

国产气已形成常规、非常规多元供气局面。2005年国内天然气产量500亿立方米，2015年增至1350亿立方米。其中，

2. China's Natural Gas Development Status

China has abundant natural gas resources. A preliminary gas supply structure is formed with a multi-type and multi-source supply pattern, which includes a mode of "West-to-East, North-to-South, Offshore Gas Going Onshore, Supply-from-Nearby". The rapid development of China's natural gas industry is supported by the stable supply and steady infrastructure construction which has begun to take shape. The natural gas consumption market has covered 31 provinces (and autonomous regions and municipalities) of Mainland China. At the same time, the marketization reform of natural gas industry is undertaking in an orderly manner and pilot projects have made phased breakthrough. These successes have laid the foundations for natural gas to become China's main energy source in the future.

(1) Great Potential of China's Natural Gas Resources

China's conventional natural gas resources are 90 Tcm, of which 50 Tcm are reserves. The shale gas resources shallower than 4500 m are 122 Tcm, of which 22 Tcm are reserves and 5.5 Tcm are currently economically recoverable. The coalbed methane resources shallower than 2000 m are 30 Tcm, of which 12.5 Tcm are reserves and 4 Tcm are currently economically recoverable.

As of the end of 2015, China's proven conventional natural gas resources were 13.01 Tcm and the remaining reserves were 5.2 Tcm. The proven resources of coalbed methane were 629.3 Bcm and its remaining reserves were 306.3 Bcm. For shale gas, the proven resources were 544.1 Bcm and the remaining reserves were 130.2 Bcm.

(2) Rapid Growth of China's Natural Gas Supply Capacity

The domestic natural gas has formed conventional and unconventional gas supply pattern. China's natural gas production was 50 Bcm in 2005 and increased to 135 Bcm in 2015. Among those, the coalbed methane production in 2015 was 4.4 Bcm, a 19% year-on-year increase. The shale gas E&P have achieved

2015年全国煤层气地面抽采量44亿立方米，同比增长19%；页岩气勘探开发自2011年获得工业性突破以来取得跨越式发展，2015年页岩气产量约46亿立方米，同比增长近3倍。

进口气已形成管道气和LNG多渠道供应格局，资源进口国达10个以上。2015年，进口气量614亿立方米，其中：管道气进口量356亿立方米，主要来自土库曼斯坦、缅甸、乌兹别克斯坦等国；LNG进口量258亿立方米，长协进口主要来自卡塔尔、澳大利亚、印度尼西亚、马来西亚和巴布亚新几内亚等国，现货进口主要来自也门、阿尔及利亚等国。

（三）中国天然气消费增长迅速

2005年中国天然气消费量为468亿立方米，2015年消费量增至1931亿立方米。2005—2015年，天然气消费年均增速16%，是中国一次能源消费年均增速的3倍。天然气在一次能源消费结构中的比例从2005年的2.4%增至2015年的5.9%，人均年用气量约140立方米。从消费结构看，2015年工业燃料消费量737亿立方米、占比38.2%，城镇燃气消费量628亿立方米、占比32.5%，发电用气量284亿立方米、占比14.7%，化工用气量282亿立方米、占比14.6%。从消费季节性特点看，受气温和用气结构的影响，不同地区季节调峰差异较大，东北、西北和环渤海地区调峰比例在12%～15%，长三角、中南地区调峰比例在5%～6%，西南、东南沿海地区调峰比例在3%～4%。天然气消费区域已扩展至中国内地31个省份（自治区、直辖市），2015年天然气消费量超过100亿立方米的省份（自治区、直辖市）有江苏、四川、新疆、广东和北京。

a great leap forward development since the industrial level production breakthrough in 2011. The shale gas production was about 4.6 Bcm in 2015, nearly a 3-fold year-on-year increase.

The imported natural gas has formed multi-source supply pattern including pipeline gas and LNG, from more than 10 importing countries. In 2015, the imported natural gas was 61.4 Bcm. Among those, the imported pipeline gas was 35.6 Bcm, mainly from Turkmenistan, Myanmar, Uzbekistan, etc. The imported LNG was 25.8 Bcm, with long-term import contracts from Qatar, Australia, Indonesia, Malaysia, Papua New Guinea and spot imports mainly from Yemen, Algeria, etc.

(3) Rapid Growth of China's Natural Gas Consumption

China's natural gas consumption was 46.8 Bcm and increased to 193.1 Bcm in 2015. From 2005 to 2015, its average annual growth rate was 16%, 3 times that of primary energy consumption rate. The proportion of natural gas in primary energy consumption structure has increased from 2.4% in 2005 to 5.9% in 2015, with 140 m^3 average annual natural gas consumption per capita. From the consumption structure aspect, the industrial fuel consumption was 73.7 Bcm, accounting for 38.2%; the urban gas consumption was 62.8 Bcm, accounting for 32.5%; natural gas consumption for power generation was 28.4 Bcm, accounting for 14.7%; while the gas consumption in the chemical industry was 28.2 Bcm, accounting for 14.6%. From the seasonal consumption characteristics aspect, as being affected by temperature and gas consumption structure, peak-load in different regions and seasons varied largely, which led to a 12%~15% of peak-load in the Northeast, Northwest and Bohai Rim regions; a 5%~6% of peak-load in the Yangtze River Delta and Central South regions and a 3%~4% of peak-load in the Southwest and Southeast Costal areas. The natural gas consumption regions have expanded to 31 provinces (autonomous regions and municipalities) of Mainland China. In 2015, Jiangsu, Sichuan, Xinjiang, Guangdong and Beijing consumed more than 10 Bcm natural.

（四）中国天然气管网基础设施处于快速发展期

截至 2015 年底，全国建成陕京线、西气东输、川气东送、中亚天然气管道、中缅天然气管道等长输管道里程约 6.4 万千米；建成 LNG 接收站 12 座，总接收能力 4380 万吨／年；建成地下储气库 18 座，有效工作气量 55 亿立方米／年；天然气发电装机容量 5700 万千瓦（不含分布式）；建成 CNG/LNG 加气站 6500 座，船用 LNG 加注站 13 座。目前已形成常规和非常规国产气、陆上进口管道气、海上进口 LNG 等多气源互济，"西气东输、北气南下、海气登陆、就近供应"的供气格局；形成地下储气库、LNG 接收站两大主力调峰方式，管网覆盖主要产气区以及长三角、珠三角和环渤海等区域。

（五）中国天然气已形成比较完整的产业体系

改革开放以来，历经多轮机构改革、企业重组等方面改革，中国天然气产业已初步形成以中国石油、中国石化、中国海油三大国有油气公司为主、其他所有制企业为辅，上游勘探开发、中游管输、下游消费市场不同程度竞争的产业格局。政府管理方面，国家发展和改革委员会、国家能源局主要负责协调全国油气行业相关政策、重大项目投资和对外合资合作等，国土资源部负责上游勘探、开发的许可管理等，国有资产监督管理委员会以出资人身份负责监管天然气行业国有企业的资产。此外，商务部、环保部、住建部、工信部、交通部、财政部、税务总局等部门按职责履行对天然气行业的管理或监管。

(4) China's Natural Gas Pipeline Network Infrastructure Under Rapid Development

As of the end of 2015, China had built Shaanxi-to-Beijing, West-to-East, Sichuan-to-East, Central Asia and Sino-Myanmar pipelines, etc., a total length of about 64 thousand kilometers; constructed 12 LNG terminals with annual receiving capacity of 43.8 million tons; built 18 underground gas storages with 5.5 Bcm annual effective working gas capacity; installed 57 million kW natural gas power generation (excluding distributed); built 6500 CNG/LNG stations and 13 marine LNG stations. So far, a multi-source natural gas supply pattern of "West-to-East, North-to-South, Offshore Gas Going Onshore, Supply-from-Nearby" has been formed, comprising of conventional and unconventional domestic gas, onshore imported pipeline gas, offshore imported LNG, etc.; two main peak-load modes using underground storages and LNG terminals have been established with pipeline network covering major gas production areas, and Yangtze River Delta, Pearl River Delta and Bohai Rim regions.

(5) A Relative Complete Industrial Structure Formed for China's Natural Gas Industry

Since the Reform and Opening-up, China's natural gas industry, after rounds of institutional reforms and corporate restructurings, has preliminarily formed a natural gas industry pattern that is grounded mainly on the three state-owned oil & gas companies, namely China National Petroleum Corporation (CNPC), China Petroleum & Chemical Corporation (Sinopec) and China National Offshore Oil Corporation (CNOOC), and supplemented by other diversified-ownership enterprises, covering the upstream E&P, midstream pipeline transportation and downstream consumer market with various levels of competitions. In government administration, National Development and Reform Commission (NDRC) and National Energy Administration (NEA) are mainly responsible for coordinating the policies relating to national oil & gas industry, major project investment and foreign joint venture cooperation, etc. Ministry of Land and Resources (MLR) governs the licensing of upstream E&P, etc. State-owned Assets Supervision and Administration Commission (SASAC) regulates the assets of state-owned enterprises in the name of investor. In addition, the relevant administration and regulation of natural gas industry are carried out by Ministry of Commerce, Ministry of Environmental Protection, Ministry of Housing and Urban-Rural Development, Ministry of Industry and Information Technology, Ministry of Transportation, Ministry of Finance, State Administration of Taxation, etc. in accordance with their responsibilities.

上游勘探开发领域参与主体逐步多元。除三大国有石油公司外，延长石油等依托既有区块参与上游勘查开采，京能、宝莫等通过新疆试点区块招投标进入上游勘探，华电、华能、重庆能投等通过招标进入页岩气上游，晋煤、河南煤层气等从事煤层气勘查开采，石化油服、长城钻探、杰瑞等多种主体参与油田服务。对外合作方面，目前中国石油、中国石化拥有陆上天然气勘探开发对外合作专营权，中国海油拥有海上专营权，中国石油、中国石化、中联煤层气公司和河南煤层气公司拥有煤层气对外合作专营权。管输领域以管输与销售捆绑垄断经营为主。目前天然气干线主要由中国石油、中国石化、中国海油等国有公司采取上中下游一体化模式管理运营，区域或省内长输管道除三大国有石油公司所建支线外，还存在与地方企业合资共建、地方管输公司或燃气公司独建等多种模式。天然气主要批发商为中国石油、中国石化和中国海油，除部分直供给电厂、工业等用户外，其余均分销给省级管网、城市燃气公司、小型LNG工厂等，然后经二次或多次销售给居民、工业、CNG加气站等终端用户。配售领域大多由地方政府授权特许经营。目前国内有超过200家城市燃气公司，2015年5大城市燃气公司（北京燃气、华润燃气、新奥燃气、中国燃气、中华煤气）合计销量相当于全国天然气销售总量的30%。

The entities participating in upstream E&P become increasingly diversified. Besides the three state-owned oil & gas companies, Yanchang Petroleum Group and other firms have participated in upstream E&P based on existing blocks where they operate; Beijing Energy Investment Holding Company, Shandong Polymer Bio-Chemical Company and others have entered into upstream E&P through Xinjiang pilot blocks bidding; China Huadian Corporation, China Huaneng Group, Chongqing Energy and others have entered the shale gas upstream business through relevant bidding process; Shanxi Jincheng Anthracite Mining Group, Henan Coalbed Methane Corporation and others have been engaged in E&P of coalbed methane; Sinopec Oilfield Service Corporation, CNPC Greatwall Drilling Company, Jereh Group and together with other entities have been involved in oilfield services. In foreign cooperation, at present, CNPC and Sinopec possess the foreign cooperation franchise of E&P of onshore natural gas resources; the offshore franchise belongs to CNOOC; CNPC, Sinopec, China United Coalbed Methane Corporation and Henan Coalbed Methane Corporation own foreign cooperation franchise of coalbed methane. The pipeline transportation field is dominated by monopoly of bundling transportation and selling. Currently, the natural gas trunk-lines are mainly administered and operated by CNPC, Sinopec, CNOOC and other state-owned enterprises in an integrated upstream, midstream and downstream mode. For the regional or provincial long distant transmission pipelines, aside from those branch lines built by the three state-owned oil companies, there are various modes of pipeline construction in terms of joint ventures with local enterprises, and solo construction by local pipeline companies or natural gas companies, etc. The major wholesalers of natural gas are CNPC, Sinopec and CNOOC. Except for the part supplied directly to power generation plants, industrial users, etc., the rest is all distributed to provincial pipeline networks, Local Distribution Company(LDC), small-size LNG plants, etc., then followed by second or multiple selling to terminal users such as residents, industries and CNG gas stations. The areas of placement are normally granted by local government using franchises. At present, there are over 200 Local Distribution Company. In 2015, the aggregated natural gas volume sold by five major Local Distribution Company(Beijing Gas, China Resources Gas, Xinao Gas, China Gas, Towngas)was 30% of the total volume of natural gas sold nation widely in 2015.

（六）中国天然气行业管理和体制政策不断完善

"十二五"以来，中国天然气领域有序开展了放开价格、放宽准入、简政放权等体制机制改革，并初步建立了产业政策体系，为未来天然气大规模发展提供了基础保障。一是完善战略、规划体系。出台了《能源发展战略行动计划（2014—2020年）》，发布了天然气、页岩气、煤层气五年期发展规划。二是勘探开发体制改革取得突破。常规油气勘探开发体制改革新疆试点完成第一轮探矿权招标，页岩气 2011 年单列为独立矿种并陆续完成了两轮探矿权招标，油气上游投资主体进一步多元化。三是落实产业政策。出台了《天然气利用政策》《页岩气产业政策》《煤层气产业政策》以及页岩气、煤层气开发利用补贴政策等。四是深化价格改革。实现了存量气、增量气价格并轨，放开了大用户直供，门站价格由政府指导定价改为基准定价，成立了上海石油天然气交易中心。五是简政放权持续推进。国内自营油气田产能建设项目全部实行备案制，非跨省（自治区、直辖市）油气管道项目、进口液化天然气接收站原址扩建项目核准权限下放到省级政府。六是加强行业管理和监管。出台了《天然气基础设施建设与运营管理办法》《油气管网设施公平开放监管办法》以及《天然气管道运输价格管理办法（试行）》《天然气管道运输定价成本监审办法（试行）》，基础设施向第三方公平开放开始实施。

(6) Continued Improvement Administration and Institutions Policies for China's Natural Gas Industry

Since "12th Five-year", institutional reforms have been carried out orderly for China's natural gas industry in areas such as price liberalization, easing market access, decentralization, etc. An industrial policy system has been preliminarily established, which provides a basic guarantee for the large-scale development of natural gas in the future. One is to improve the strategy and planning system. "Energy Development Strategic Action Plan (2014-2020)" has been released and five-year development plans for natural gas, shale gas and coalbed methane have been issued. Two is to make breakthrough in E&P system reform. Conventional oil and gas E&P system reform pilot in Xinjiang completed the first round of exploration tender; shale gas was categorized as a new independent mineral in 2011 and two rounds of shale gas right of exploration tenders have completed, further diversifying the oil & gas upstream investment subjects. Three is to implement the industrial policies. "Natural Gas Utilization Policy" "Shale Gas Industry Policy", "Coalbed Methane Industry Policy" and shale gas, coalbed methane development and utilization subsidy policy, etc. have been released. Four is to deepen the price reform. The prices of stock gas and incremental gas have been merged; the control over direct supply to large consumers has been lifted; the government guidance pricing for city-gate gas has been altered to benchmark pricing; Shanghai Petroleum and Natural Gas Exchange Center has been established. Five is to continue to promote decentralization. The filling system has been implemented in all domestic oil and gas field capacity building projects; the approval authorities have been decentralized to provincial government for provincial oil and gas pipeline projects and imported LNG terminals sites expansion projects. Six is to strengthen the industrial administration and regulation. "Measures for the Administration of Natural Gas Infrastructure Construction and Operation", "Measures for the Supervision and Administration of Fair Opening of Oil and Gas Pipelines Network Facilities", "Measures for the Administration of Natural Gas Pipeline Transportation Price (for Trial Implementation)" and "Measures for the Supervision and Examination of Natural Gas Pipeline Transportation Pricing Cost" have been introduced; the equal opening of infrastructure construction to Third Party Access has been implemented.

三、中国天然气发展前景

随着中国生态文明建设的持续推进，新型工业化、城镇化深入发展，天然气产业迎来了难得的发展机遇。通过推动能源革命，深化体制机制改革，加强国际合作，未来中国将形成市场结构合理、资源供应多元、储运设施完善、法律法规健全的统一开放、竞争有序的现代天然气产业体系，天然气将逐步成为中国的主体能源。

（一）中国天然气市场需求潜力大

2015年，中国人均天然气消费量约140立方米，天然气占一次能源消费总量的比重约5.9%，远低于世界平均水平的23.7%。随着中国绿色低碳能源战略的持续推进，发展清洁低碳能源将成为优化能源结构的重要途径，未来较长一段时期天然气将在中国能源发展中扮演重要角色。通过加大政策支持力度，力争2020年天然气在一次能源消费结构中的占比达到10%；到2030年，力争将天然气在一次能源消费中的占比提高到15%左右。未来天然气需求增量主要来自城镇燃气、天然气发电、工业燃料和交通运输四大领域。

城镇燃气：随着中国新型城镇化建设深入推进，城镇化率稳步提升，预计到2020年达60%，2030年达70%。未来城镇燃气发展方向主要包括三个方面：一是稳步发展民用气。提升居民气化水平，城镇居民气化率2020年达50%～55%，2030年达65%～70%，并同步拓展公共服务、商业用气市场。二是

3. China's Natural Gas Development Prospects

With the continuous advance of China's ecological civilization construction, new industrialization and urbanization, its natural gas industry has ushered a rare opportunity for development. By promoting energy revolution, deepening the reform of institutional mechanisms, and strengthening international cooperation, China will form a unified and open, competitive and orderly modern natural gas industry system with reasonable market structure, diversified resource supply, multiple storage facilities and sound laws and regulations. Natural gas will gradually become the main energy source for China.

(1) Potentially Large Demand of China's Natural Gas Market

In 2015, China's natural gas consumption per capita was about 140 m^3, accounting for about 5.9% of its total primary energy consumption, which is far below the world average level of 23.7%. With the continuous advance of China's green low-carbon energy strategy, the development of clean low-carbon energy will become an important way to optimize its energy structure. For a long period in the future of China, natural gas will play an important role in its energy development. By increasing policy support efforts, it is strive to grow the proportion of natural gas in primary energy consumption structure to 10% in 2020. By 2030, the proportion of natural gas in primary energy consumption will be targeted to increase to about 15%. The future demand for natural gas mainly will come from four major areas: urban gas, natural gas for power generation, industrial fuel and transportation.

Urban gas: with the deepening of China's new urbanization, urbanization rate steadily increases, which is expected to reach 60% in 2020 and 70% in 2030. The future direction of the development of urban gas mainly includes three aspects: one is the steady development of domestic gas. By upgrading the level of resident gasification, urban resident gasification rate will reach 50%~55% in 2020 and 65%~70% in 2030, while synchronizing the

有序发展天然气采暖。发展城市集中式采暖、燃气空调、分户式采暖，在南方有条件地区以集中式和分散式供暖相结合的方式利用天然气采暖。三是推进重点地区气化。以京津冀及周边地区、长三角、珠三角、东北地区等为重点，设立重点区域"禁煤区"，加快燃煤锅炉天然气替代以及城市、乡镇生活燃料以气代煤。

天然气发电： 天然气发电既是电源结构的重要组成部分，也是天然气市场发展的主要驱动力。目前，中国天然气发电呈现装机和发电量"双低"状态。未来中国天然气发电的发展方向主要包括三个方面：一是有序发展天然气调峰电站，提升能源融合水平。促进天然气发电与可再生能源发电融合发展和提升用电负荷中心电力安全保障水平。二是因地制宜发展天然气热电联产，提升环境质量。在大气污染防治重点地区的经济技术开发区、高新产业园区鼓励发展带稳定热负荷的热电联产项目，在采暖地区适度发展带采暖的热电联产项目。三是大力发展天然气分布式能源，提升能源品质。在大中城市的大型商业综合服务区、高校园区及高新产业园区等加快发展天然气分布式能源，提升天然气综合利用效率。预计到2020年，天然气发电装机占中国电源总装机达到5%以上；到2030年，力争将天然气发电装机比例提高到10%左右。

工业燃料： 目前，欧美等发达国家工业燃料中煤炭占比低于15%，而中国高达70%以上。2015年中国工业燃料用能中，天然气占比仅为10%，远低于欧美日等发达国家水平（40%～50%）。为实现中国工业燃料质量升级，必须对工业

development of public services and commercial gas market. Two is the orderly development of natural gas for heating. Urban central heating, gas air conditioning, household-based heating, and the combination of centralized and decentralized heating using natural gas in the South China area where possible will be developed. Three is the promotion of gasification in key areas. In Jing-Jin-Ji and surrounding area, Yangtze River Delta, Pearl River Delta, Northeast Region and other key areas, key regional "No Coal Zone" will be established to accelerate the "Coal-to-Gas" for coal-fired boiler as well as urban and rural fuel.

Natural gas power generation: natural gas power generation is not only an important part of the power structure, but also the main driving force for the development of natural gas market. At present, China's natural gas power generation installed capacity and electrical output are both low. The future direction of the development of China's natural gas power generation mainly includes three aspects: one is the orderly development of natural gas peak-load stations to improve the level of energy integration. China will promote the integration of natural gas power generation and renewable energy power generation and enhance the level of security of electricity load centers. Two is the development of natural gas fired cogeneration in accordance with local conditions, in order to improve the environmental quality. China will encourage the development of cogeneration projects with stable thermal load and heating projects in heating areas in the economic and technological development zones as well as high-tech industrial parks in the key air pollution control areas. Three is the rigorous development of natural gas distributed energy and improvement of energy quality. China will accelerate the development of natural gas distributed energy to enhance the comprehensive utilization efficiency of natural gas, in the integrated commercial service areas, university parks and high-tech industrial parks of large and medium-sized cities. It is expected by 2020 to realize 5% of China's total installed capacity being natural gas power generation; and by 2030, to strive to increase this proportion to about 10%.

Industrial fuel: At present, in Europe, United States and other developed countries, coal accounts for less than 15% in industrial fuels, while this proportion for China is more than 70%. In 2015, China's natural gas only accounted for 10% of its industrial fuel mix, far below the level of Europe, United States, Japan and other developed countries (40%~50%). In order to

领域的能源结构进行调整,"煤改气"是切实有效的措施之一。未来天然气在工业燃料领域的发展方向主要包括两个方面:一是优化钢铁、冶金、建材、石化等耗能行业的燃料构成,二是改善城市中不同工业锅炉、窑炉的燃料结构。预计到 2020 年,天然气占工业燃料能源消费量的比例达到 15%;到 2030 年,力争将天然气占工业燃料能源消费量的比例提高到 25% 左右。

交通运输:2015 年中国天然气汽车保有量约 500 万辆,用气量超过 200 亿立方米。交通运输行业是中国节能减排和应对气候变化的重点领域之一,发展天然气车船是加快推进绿色低碳交通运输较为现实的选择。未来天然气车船发展方向主要包括三个方面:一是推广使用 LNG 载货汽车。在公路网络完善、物流发达、减排任务重的地区发展 LNG 重卡;在港口、物流园区、矿区、厂区等区域优先使用天然气汽车;鼓励城市物流车辆发展 LNG 轻卡。二是推进城市公共交通行业"油改气"。加快发展城市天然气公交车和城际天然气客车,提高公交车的气化率;鼓励发展城市 CNG 出租车,并加快向中小城市推广。三是推进水运行业"油改气"。发展内河、港口区域作业 LNG 动力船舶,试点推广沿海 LNG 动力船舶;鼓励干散货船、滚装船、拖船等以旧换新、新购单燃料 LNG 动力船舶。预计到 2020 年,实现气化车辆 1000 万辆,气化船舶 6 万艘;到 2030 年,力争实现气化车辆 1400 万辆,气化船舶 8 万艘。

(二)中国天然气资源供应持续增长

未来中国天然气供应构成主体多元、国内与国外并重的资源保障体系。预计到 2020 年,中国天然气供应能力达到 3600

realize the upgrading of China's industrial fuel quality, it is necessary to adjust the industrial energy structure with "Coal-to-Gas" as one of the feasible and effective measures. The future direction of developing natural gas in industrial fuels mainly includes two aspects: one is the optimization of the industrial fuel structure for iron and steel, metallurgy, building materials, petrochemical and other energy consuming industries; two is the improvement of the fuel structure of different urban industrial boilers and furnaces. It is expected by 2020, natural gas will account for 15% of industrial fuel consumption; and by 2030, to strive to increase this proportion to about 25%.

Transportation: China's natural gas vehicle quantity was about 5 million in 2015 with natural gas consumption over 20 Bcm. Transportation industry is one of the key areas of energy saving, emission reduction and climate change control in China. The development of natural gas vehicles and vessels is a more realistic choice to accelerate green and low-carbon transportation. The future direction of the development of natural gas vehicles and vessels mainly includes three aspects: one is the promotion of LNG trucks. China will develop LNG heavy trucks in places having developed highway network and logistics with critical emission reduction target; prioritize the use of natural gas vehicles at the ports, logistics parks, mining areas and industrial plant areas; and encourage LNG light trucks as city logistics vehicles. Two is the promotion of "Oil-to-Gas" in urban public transportation. China will speed up the development of natural gas urban and intercity buses to improve the bus gasification rate; and encourage the development of urban CNG taxis and accelerate the promotion toward small and medium cities. Three is the promotion of "Oil-to-Gas" in waterway transportation. China will develop LNG vessels in inland waterways and port areas, and pilot to promote coastal LNG vessels; and encourage the replacement of bulk carriers, ro-ro ships and tugboats with single fuel LNG vessels. It is expected to achieve 10 million gasified vehicles and 60 thousand gasified vessels by 2020; and to strive to increase these quantities to 14 million and 80 thousand by 2030, respectively.

(2) Continued Growth of Natural Gas Supply

China's future natural gas supply shall establish a diversified resources security system, emphasizing on both domestic and foreign resources. Expected by 2020, China's natural gas supply capacity will reach upwards of

亿立方米以上。到 2030 年，中国天然气供应能力达 6000 亿立方米以上。

加大国内资源勘探开发，保持产量较快增长。按照"海陆并重、常非并举"的原则，鼓励各类社会资本进入，在加强常规天然气勘探开发的同时，加快推进页岩气、煤层气等非常规天然气规模效益开发，形成有效产能接替。

加快常规天然气增储上产步伐。陆上常规天然气以四川、鄂尔多斯、塔里木等盆地为重点，强化已开发气田稳产，做好已探明未开发储量、新增探明储量开发评价和产能建设工作。加大深层天然气勘探开发力度，拓展增产空间；加快鄂尔多斯、四川等盆地低渗—致密气上产步伐。海域成为未来天然气主要增储上产区之一，加强深水领域天然气勘探开发，拓展深水增储空间。

加强页岩气高效开发，推进快速上产增储。以四川盆地及周缘等南方海相页岩气为重点，全面突破海相页岩气高效开发技术，推广应用水平井、"工厂化"作业模式，降本增效，实现产量大幅增长；探索南华北、贵州等海陆过渡相和鄂尔多斯、辽河等陆相页岩气勘探开发潜力，寻找新的核心区。

推进煤层气规模效益开发。立足沁水盆地南部、鄂尔多斯东缘煤层气产业基地，实现规模效益开发；加快二连盆地、准噶尔盆地东部、蜀南、黑龙江东部、贵州等地区煤层气勘探评价，扩大资源后备阵地。

有序开展资源引进工作，保障稳定供应。根据中国天然气市场形势变化，有序采购进口天然气资源，管道气与 LNG 并重，长、短期合同与现货结合，鼓励各类社会资本参与。

360 Bcm. By 2030, this capacity will reach 600 Bcm and more.

Increase E&P of domestic resources to maintain a rapid output growth. In accordance with the "Onshore-Offshore and Conventional-Unconventional" principle, China encourages all kind of social capital investment and accelerates the effective and scaled shale gas, coalbed methane and other unconventional gas development at the same time of strengthening the conventional gas E&P, in order to form an effective production capacity replacement.

Speed up conventional natural gas reserves and production enhancement. With onshore conventional natural gas in Sichuan, Ordos, Tarim and other basins as the focus, production in developed gas fields will be strengthened to maintain, and evaluation and production capacity building of proven undeveloped and newly added proven reserves will be carried out in the right way. China will increase the efforts in deep natural gas E&P to expand production enhancement space; and accelerate low permeability and tight gas production pace in Ordos, Sichuan and other basins. Offshore has become one of the main areas to increase natural gas reserves and production in the future. China will reinforce the E&P of deepwater gas field, expanding the deepwater reserve growth space.

Strengthen efficient development of shale gas and promote the rapid growth of production and reserves. In Sichuan basin and its surrounding southern marine shale gas plays, comprehensive technology breakthrough will be made in highly effective marine shale gas development, and horizontal well and "factory" operation model will be promoted in order to reduce cost and increase efficiency to achieve substantial growth. China will explore for new core areas in the southern part of North China, Guizhou and other transitional shale plays as well as Ordos, Liaohe and other continental shale plays.

Promote scaled and efficient development of coalbed methane. Based on the southern Qinshui Basin and the eastern margin of Ordos coalbed methane industrial base, scaled and efficient development is aimed to be achieved. The exploration and evaluation of Erenhot Basin, Eastern Junggar Basin, Southern Sichuan, Eastern Heilongjiang, Guizhou, etc. will be accelerated to expand reserves.

Orderly carry out resources importation to ensure stable supply. According to China's natural gas market changes, natural gas importation will be orderly procured, emphasizing both on pipeline gas and LNG, combining long, short-term contracts and spot gas, encouraging all kinds of social capital participation.

(三)中国天然气输配体系明显完善

根据天然气资源来源和市场需求分布情况,中国将长期维持"西气东输、北气南下、海气登陆、就近供应"的天然气流向,并据此构建天然气管网体系,形成连接四大进口战略通道,以西气东输系统、陕京线系统、川气东送系统、西南管网系统、中俄东线系统和沿海通道为骨架的纵横交错、覆盖全国的供气管网系统并且"区内成网、区域连通、气源多元、调运灵活、供应稳定"的供气格局。

预计到2020年,中国天然气长输管道总里程10万～12万千米,一次管输能力3700亿～4000亿立方米/年。全国地级及以上城市管网覆盖率90%以上,县级城市管网覆盖率60%以上,覆盖重点乡镇和工业园区。预计到2030年,中国天然气长输管道总里程17万～20万千米,一次管输能力6000亿～7000亿立方米/年。全国地级及以上城市覆盖率95%以上,县级城市管网覆盖率80%以上,持续提高乡镇和工业园区的管网覆盖率。

未来中国天然气管道建设重点围绕进口通道、外输干线、区域联络线和"最后一公里"管道等四方面展开。一是视资源落实和市场开发,进一步构建和完善进口通道。依托俄罗斯东部天然气(蒙古国煤制天然气资源待落实),构建东北通道,形成连通东北、环渤海和长三角区域的东部干线管网。依托中亚国家天然气(俄罗斯西部资源待落实),持续增强环渤海、长三角区域的供气能力。依托海上进口天然气资源,加强LNG接收站间的互连互通,提高沿海互济供气能力。二是根据西南

(3) Clear Improvement of China's Natural Gas Transmission and Distribution System

According to the source of natural gas supply and distribution of market demand, China will maintain a long-term natural gas transmission direction in terms of "West-to-East, North-to-South, Offshore Gas Going Onshore, Supply-from-Nearby", and construct the natural gas pipeline network system accordingly. A "intra-regionally networked, inter-regionally connected, multi-source, flexible and stable" gas supplying pattern covering the whole country will be formed, which connects the four strategic import channels and crisscrosses the West-to-East gas pipeline, the Shannxi-Beijing line system, the Sichuan-East Gas Transmission system, the Southwest Pipeline system, the East Sino-Russia system, and the Coastal channel.

Expected by 2020, the total mileage of China's natural gas pipeline will reach 100~120 thousand km, with annual transmission capacity of 370~400 Bcm. The network coverage percentage will be over 90% in cities at prefecture level or above. In county level cities, this percentage will be 60%, covering key townships and industrial parks. Expected by 2030, the total mileage will reach 170~200 thousand kilometers, with annual transmission capacity of 600~700 Bcm. The network coverage percentage will be over 90% in cities at prefecture level or above. In county level cities, this percentage will be 60%, continuously improving the coverage for the townships and industrial parks.

China's future natural gas pipeline construction will focus on four aspects, namely, the import channels, external transport lines, regional tie lines and "end-user distribution network" pipelines. One is to further build and improve the strategical channels based on the status of resources and market development. Relying on Eastern Russia natural gas, China will construct the northeast channel, forming an eastern pipeline network connecting the Northeast, Bohai Rim and Yangtze River Delta regions. Depending on natural gas resources in Central Asia, the gas supply capacity to Bohai Rim and Yangtze River Delta regions will be continuously enhanced. Based on offshore importation of natural gas, the interconnection and intercommunication among LNG terminals will be strengthened to improve the coastal mutual supply capacity. Two is to timely construct supporting external transmission lines and enhance the supply capacity based on the Southwest conventional

地区常规气、页岩气上产节奏以及新疆和内蒙古煤制天然气项目建设进度，适时建设配套外输干线，增强供气能力。三是大力建设干线联络线、区域联络线和枢纽站，以进一步提高全国和区域天然气管网网络化程度，提升管网利用率，增强调运灵活性，保障供应可靠性，带动区域协调发展。四是加强省内干线和支线管道建设力度，统筹规划、分步实施，最终形成通达全省、覆盖各市的多进多出、互连互通、设施完备、保障有力的省内天然气输配网络。

（四）中国天然气综合性的调峰体系有序建立

中国未来将主要依托枯竭油气藏继续建设地下储气库，形成环渤海、东北、长三角、西南、中部和中南六大区域联网协调的储气库群，到2020年，形成有效工作气量148亿立方米，到2030年，形成有效工作气量300亿立方米。根据全国各消费区域资源流向和市场实际需求情况，结合港口规划统筹优化沿海LNG接收站布局。在天然气需求量大、应急调峰能力要求高的环渤海、长三角、东南沿海地区，优先扩大已建LNG接收站储转能力，适度新建LNG接收站，最终形成1亿吨／年以上的总接收能力。此外，在用气负荷中心城市，加快建设小型LNG储罐、CNG高压管束、天然气球罐及其他配套储气调峰设施，以解决重点城市的日调峰、小时调峰和应急状况时的保供要求。经过10年到20年的努力，中国逐步建立以地下储气库群和LNG接收站储罐调峰为主，气田、CNG和LNG储备站调峰为辅，可中断用户为补充的应急调峰设施，建立健全由供气方、输配企业和用户各自承担责任的综合性调峰体系。

gas and shale gas production as well as Xinjiang and Inner Mongolia coal gasification project progress. Three is to construct trunk lines, tie lines and hubs to further increase the national and regional natural gas pipeline network level, improve network utilization, enhance the transmission flexibility, ensure supply reliability, and promote regional coordinated development. Four is to reinforce the intra-provincial trunk and branch pipeline construction, overall planning, and step-by-step implementation to ultimately form an interconnected and intercommunicated, complete, and powerful intra-provincial natural gas pipeline network covering all the cities.

(4) Orderly Establishment of China's Comprehensive Natural Gas Peak-load System

China in future will continue to construct underground gas storages mainly based on depleted oil and gas reservoirs, forming connected and coordinated gas storage groups comprised of six regions, namely, Bohai Rim, Northeast, Yangtze River Delta, Southwest, Central, and Central South, with annual effective working gas capacity of 14.8 Bcm by 2020 and 30 Bcm by 2030. According to the resources flow direction and actual market demand of the consuming regions, as well as port planning, the costal LNG terminals distributions will be optimized. In Bohai Rim, Yangtze River Delta and Southeast Costal areas with great natural gas demand and high emergent peak-load requirement, expansion of storage capability of existing LNG terminals will be prioritized with a reasonable number of new LNG terminals to be built, eventually forming a total annual receiving capacity of 100 million tons. In addition, in gas load center cities, small LNG storage tanks, CNG high pressure tubes, natural gas spherical tanks and other auxiliary gas peak-load facilities will be constructed in an accelerated pace, in order to solve the daily peak-load, hour peak-load and emergency situations in key cities. With 10 to 20 years of efforts, China will gradually establish emergency peak-load facilities dominated by underground gas storage groups and LNG terminals storage peak-load and supplemented by gas fields, CNG and LNG storage stations with capability to terminate supply to users to complement emergent needs, and develop a comprehensive peak-load system with responsibilities borne by gas suppliers, transmission and distribution enterprises and end users, respectively.

四、中国天然气战略地位、发展路径和政策取向

新形势下世界能源清洁低碳的发展方向和中国能源发展战略对中国加快天然气产业发展提出了更高要求。破解制约天然气产业发展的体制性和结构性问题，强化环保、财税等政策支持，积极推进试点、示范，实现中国天然气产业快速、健康、可持续发展。

（一）将天然气发展为中国主体能源之一

天然气是一种高效、低碳、清洁的优质能源。在发电和工业燃料领域，天然气热效率比煤炭高约10%，天然气冷热电三联供热效率较燃煤发电高近1倍。天然气二氧化碳排放量是煤炭的59%、燃料油的72%。大型燃气—蒸汽联合循环机组二氧化硫排放浓度几乎为零，工业锅炉上二氧化硫排放量天然气是煤炭的17%、燃料油的25%；大型燃气—蒸汽联合循环机组氮氧化物排放量是超低排放煤电机组的73%，工业锅炉的氮氧化物排放量天然气是煤炭的20%；另外，与煤炭、燃料油相比，天然气无粉尘排放。

燃气电厂具有极优的调节和响应能力，可与可再生能源形成良性互补。可再生能源受技术、成本、储能等多种因素的制约，客观上需要相当规模的灵活调节电源与之相匹配。燃气电厂具有启停迅速、运行灵活的特点，气电与风电或光伏发电建立有机配合的"风气互补"或"光气互补"联合机组，可有效解决目前的弃风、弃光问题，提升发电机组的总出力水平和电网运

4. China's Natural Gas Development: Strategic Positioning, Growth Pathway and Policy Orientation

Under the new situation, the development direction of the world's clean and low-carbon energy and the strategy of China's energy development put forward higher requirement for China to accelerate the development of its natural gas industry. China will crack the institutional and structural restrictions on its natural gas industry, strengthen the environmental protection, taxation and other policy supports, and actively promote the pilots, demonstration, to achieve rapid, healthy and sustainable development of China's natural gas industry.

(1) Developing Natural Gas as One of the Main Energy Source in China

Natural gas is a low-carbon and clean high-quality energy. The thermal efficiency of natural gas is about 10% higher than that of coal in power generation and industrial fuels. Its thermal efficiency of the total energy system is nearly one times higher than that of coal-fired power generation. Carbon dioxide emissions from natural gas are 59% of coal and 72% of fuel oil. Sulfur dioxide emissions of large gas-steam combined cycle unit are almost zero and those of industrial boiler using natural gas are 17% of coal and 25% of fuel oil. Nitrogen oxide emissions of large gas-steam combined cycle unit are 73% of the ultra-low emission coal power units and those of industrial boiler are 20% of coal. In addition, compared with coal and fuel oil, natural gas is dust-free.

Gas power plants have excellent adaptability and responding capability, which can form a positive complementarity with renewable energy. With the constraints of technology, cost, energy storage and other factors, renewable energy needs a considerable size of flexible power supply to match. Gas power plants have the characteristics of rapid start-and-stop and flexible operation. "Wind-Gas Hybrid" or "Solar-Gas Hybrid" combined units can effectively solve the current "wind curtailment" and "solar curtailment" problems to improve the total output of the power units and the operating reliability of the power grids. Therefore, it is an important way for China to

行可靠性，因此与天然气协同发展成为中国未来大规模发展风电和光伏发电的重要途径。

天然气资源丰富、供应充足、成本相对低廉、使用便利、节能减排效果显著，大力发展天然气，有助于实现清洁低碳、环境友好的新型城镇化发展目标，满足人民群众的新期盼。中国仍处于工业化和城镇化加速发展阶段，随着新型城镇化的推进和人们生活水平的提高，清洁低碳的能源需求将持续增长，通过创新能源发展道路，转变以煤炭为主的能源结构，大规模利用天然气，破解土壤、水、大气污染等生态环境瓶颈约束，以保障食物安全、饮用水安全、生态安全和人居环境安全，大大提高人们的生活水平和生活品质，为全面建成小康社会提供有力支撑。

天然气是中国优化能源结构、推进节能减排、治理大气污染、建设美丽城镇等方面最为现实的选择。应大力发展天然气产业，大幅度提高天然气消费比重，逐步把天然气培育成为中国的主体能源。力争到2030年，天然气占中国一次能源消费的比重达到15%左右，成为继煤炭、石油之后的第三大主体能源。

（二）构建统一开放的天然气市场体系

有序放开天然气上游领域。坚持油气矿业权国家一级管理，逐步有序放开勘查开采市场准入条件，公开公平向符合条件的市场主体竞争性出让矿业权，逐步形成以大型国有油气公司为主导、多种市场主体共同参与的勘探开发市场体系。完善区块退出机制。加强政府对地质资料的汇交管理，优化和加强国家

develop large scale wind power and solar power in the future with the co-development of natural gas.

Natural gas has the advantages of abundant resources, ample supplies, relatively low cost, convenient use and remarkable energy saving and emission reduction effects. Therefore, vigorous development of natural gas helps to achieve a clean low-carbon and environmentally friendly new urbanization development goal and meet the new expectations of the people. As China is still in the accelerated development stage of industrialization and urbanization, with the new urbanization and the improvement of people's living standards, clean low-carbon energy demand will continue to grow. Through the innovative energy development path, natural gas will be used to change the coal-dominated energy structure and break the bottleneck of ecological environment, such as soil, water and air pollution, in order to ensure food, drinking water, ecological and human settlement securities, which will greatly improve people's living standard and life quality and provide a strong support for building the well-off society in an all-round way.

Natural gas is the most realistic choice for China to optimize the energy structure, promote energy conservation and emission reduction, control the air pollution, and construct beautiful towns, etc. China should vigorously develop its natural gas industry by significantly improving the proportion of natural gas consumption and gradually turning natural gas as China's main energy source. By 2030, natural gas will be strived to grow to be 15% of China's primary energy consumption and will become the third main energy source after coal and oil.

(2) Building a Unified and Open Market System for Natural Gas

Orderly open the natural gas upstream market. Adhering to the national level administration of oil and oil mining rights, the market access conditions to the E&P business will be gradually released in an orderly manner; mining rights will be transferred to qualified market players openly and fairly. An E&P market system will be gradually formed, dominated by large state-owned oil and gas companies and supplemented by the participation of a variety of market players. Block withdrawal mechanism will be improved. Geological data submitting management by government will be reinforced and the national

财政支持的地质普查和其他公益性勘查资料及成果的利用和共享。

落实基础设施第三方公平准入。有序推进天然气长输管道（含干线、支干线、省际和省内管网等）和城镇燃气管道运输与销售分离，将实行独立核算或具有独立法人资格作为管道运营的基本条件，为第三方公平接入提供前提。鼓励社会资本参与或组建混合所有制企业开展管道、LNG 接收站、储气库等基础设施投资建设，为第三方公平接入夯实基础。完善油气管网监管体系、质量标准体系、管线接入标准，加强管网规划、建设和运营信息公开，为第三方公平接入完善规制。依据市场化原则，合理消化已签订的长约协议，鼓励企业参与天然气进口，拓宽进口渠道。

建立多层次的现代天然气市场体系。重点推进上海、重庆等天然气交易中心建设，形成公平规范的现货期货市场交易平台，在交易规则、交易程序和交易范围上逐步与国际接轨，逐步形成全国统一的天然气交易市场，形成由不同区域价格构成的全国天然气价格体系和天然气市场流通格局。健全天然气市场信用体系，建立守信激励和失信惩戒机制，加强对失信主体的惩戒和约束。探索商业服务模式创新，推进"互联网+"智慧天然气系统建设，有序构建涵盖上游开采、中游输配、下游消费的全产业链数据共享平台。

推进改革试点示范。积极探索、试点先行，着力加强重点领域、关键环节改革，探索一批可持续、可推广的试点经验。一是扩大勘探开发改革试点范围。在常规油气勘探开发体制改

financial support for the use and sharing of geological survey and other public geological prospecting data will be optimized and strengthened.

Implement fair Third Party Access(TPA) to infrastructure. In order to provide the premise for the fair Third Party Access, the separation between long distance natural gas pipeline transportation and urban gas pipeline transportation/sales will be promoted in an orderly manner; independent account or possessing independent legal entity will be implemented as the basic conditions for pipeline operation. Social capital or mixed ownership enterprises will be encouraged to carry out pipelines, LNG terminals, gas storage and other infrastructure investment and construction, laying down a solid foundation for the fair Third Party Access. Oil and gas pipeline network supervision system, quality standard system, pipeline access standards will be improved. Information disclosure of the pipeline network planning, construction and operation will be reinforced to perfect the regulation for the fair Third Party Access. According to the principle of marketization, the long-term contract will be reasonably digested; enterprises'participation in natural gas importation will be encouraged, broadening the import channels.

Establish a multi-level modern natural gas market system. Focusing on promoting the construction of Shanghai, Chongqing and other natural gas trading centers, a fair trading platform for the spot futures market will be built. With the gradual internationalization of trading rules, procedures and ranges, a unified national natural gas market will be gradually formed, realizing a national natural gas price system and market circulation pattern comprised by different regional prices. The natural gas market credit system will be perfected by establishing the trustworthy incentives and dishonesty disciplinary mechanisms, and strengthening the punishment and restraint of entities losing faith. New business service model innovation will be explored and "Internet Plus" smart natural gas system will be promoted, to orderly construct a whole industry chain data sharing platform covering the upstream development, midstream transmission and distribution, and downstream consumption.

Promote pilot demonstration of reforms. Through active exploring and piloting, reforms in key areas and links will be specially reinforced, to explore a number of sustainable and scalable pilot experience. One is to expand the scope of E&P reform pilot. On the basis of the pilot reform of conventional oil

革新疆试点基础上总结经验向全国推广，完善页岩气、煤层气探矿权公开招标制度。二是有序推进综合性改革试点。支持新疆能源综合改革，支持重庆、江苏、上海等省市开展天然气体制改革试点，推进云南省保山市天然气利用试验示范区建设。三是推进天然气管道、LNG 接收站等基础实施第三方开放试点，为全国范围内全面推行第三方公平准入探索规则、积累经验。四是开展配套改革试点，包括天然气价格放开、城镇燃气特许经营改革试点等。五是推进分布式、光气互补、风气互补、互联网＋、LNG 江海联运等重点领域试点示范，破解新兴领域发展的体制机制障碍，拓展天然气发展空间。

（三）形成市场化的天然气价格机制

放开竞争性环节价格。按照"管住中间，放开两端"的原则，尽快全面放开气源价格、城市门站价格和终端销售价格。修订天然气计量计价方式，由流量或质量计量计价改为能量（热值）计量计价。建立完善季节性气价、峰谷气价以及储气价实施办法。理顺居民生活用气价格，遵循基本市场规律，取消民用、非民用气价交叉补贴，按照供气实际成本确定不同用量的居民用气价格，保留对生活困难人群和特殊群体的适当补贴或救助机制，"暗补"变"明补"。最终建立与中国天然气资源禀赋特点和天然气产业发展阶段相适应，真实反映时间、空间、品质特性的天然气价格形成机制，体现供气成本、市场供需和用户多样化需求。

加强输配环节政府定价及监管。政府按"准许成本加合理收益"原则，对具有自然垄断性质的输气和配气环节，分级分

and gas E&P system in Xinjiang Province, the experience will be promoted nation widely to improve the public bidding system for shale gas and coalbed methane exploration rights. Two is to orderly promote the comprehensive reform pilot. China supports the energy comprehensive reform in Xinjiang and natural gas system reform pilot in Chongqing, Jiangsu, Shanghai and other provinces and municipalities, and promotes the construction of natural gas utilization test demonstration zone in Boshan city of Yunnan. Three is to promote the third party access pilot to natural gas pipeline, LNG terminals and other infrastructures, to explore rules and accumulate experience for fully implementation of the fair Third Party Access nation widely. Four is to carry out coordinated reform pilot, including natural gas price liberalization, the pilot reform of urban gas franchise, etc. Five is to promote the distributed, solar-gas hybrid, wind-gas hybrid, Internet Plus, LNG river-ocean combined transportation and other key areas of pilot demonstration, break the barriers of institutional mechanisms for development of new areas, and expand the space for natural gas development.

(3) Establishing Market-based Pricing Mechanisms of Natural Gas

Liberalize the prices in competitive sectors. According to the principle of "controlling the middle, liberalizing the two ends", prices of the upstream and source gas, at city-gate station and the terminal sale will be liberalized as soon as possible. The natural gas metering and pricing method will be revised from flow or mass basis to thermal basis. The implementation of seasonal gas price, peak gas price and storage gas price will be established and improved. China will straighten out the residential gas price, follow the basic market rules, abolish the cross-subsidy of the civil and non-civil gas prices, determine usage-based different residential gas prices according to the actual gas supply cost, and retain the appropriate subsidies or assistance mechanism for people living in difficult and special groups, turning "invisible subsidy" to "visible subsidy". Finally, a natural gas pricing mechanism, which adapts to China's natural gas resources characteristics and natural gas industry development stage as well as truly reflects the time, space, and quality characteristics of natural gas, will be established, embodying the supply cost, market supply and demand, and diverse user needs.

Strengthen government regulation of transmission and distribution prices. In accordance with the pricing principle of "permitted cost plus

类制定跨省、省内管道运输价格、城镇燃气配气价格及具体管理办法，并建立相应的价格调整机制。加强对管网投资、运维成本监审，加强信息公开。各地需加强省内管道运输价格和配气价格监管，降低过高的省内管道运输价格和配气价格。减少供气中间环节，鼓励大用户管输直供。规范清理天然气输配企业各项收费，努力降低终端用气成本。

（四）强化天然气行业管理及监管

完善法律法规体系。在单行法方面，研究制定《石油天然气法》或《天然气法》，规范资源所有权、行业准入、管理职责和分工、发展规划、生产作业许可、管道运营及公平接入、环境保护、科技创新、国际合作、税费制度、油气储备等。在专项法方面，修订《矿产资源法》《对外合作开采陆上石油资源条例》《对外合作开采海洋石油资源条例》《天然气利用政策》等，使其更适应新形势下天然气勘查、生产、输送、储配和利用等各环节特点。通过司法解释等途径处理好《石油天然气管道保护法》与其他法律之间的冲突等。

加强行业监管。建立覆盖全产业链、全过程的天然气监管体系，加强政府对市场准入、交易行为、垄断环节、税收缴纳、价格成本、质量、安全、环保等重点环节的监管。加快完善天然气产业标准化体系。重视信息公开和社会监管，发挥社会组织和第三方机构的社会监督和桥梁作用以及媒体在宣传环保知识和披露违法违规行为等方面的积极作用。

reasonable profit", China will classify and formulate the inter-province and intra-province pipeline transport prices, urban gas distribution prices and specific management measures to the links which have the monopolistic nature on the gas transmission and distribution. It will strengthen the supervision and examination of pipeline network investment and operating cost, and reinforce information disclosure. All local governments should strengthen their supervision on intra-provincial pipeline transport price and distribution price and lower the relevant prices. The intermediate links of gas supply will be reduced and direct transmission to large users will be encouraged. Efforts will be taken to reduce the cost of terminal gas by regulating and cleaning up various charges to natural gas transmission and distribution enterprises.

(4) Strengthening Management and Regulation of Natural Gas Industry

Improve the legal and regulatory system. In the aspect of separate law, the "Oil and Natural Gas Law" or "Natural Gas Law" will be formulated to regulate resource ownership, market access, administration responsibility and division, development planning, operating licensing, pipeline operation and fair access, environmental protection, technology innovation, international cooperation, taxation system, oil and gas storage, etc. For special law, the "Mineral Resource Law", "Regulations on Sino-foreign Cooperation in the Development of Continental Petroleum Resources", "Regulation on the Exploitation of Offshore Petroleum Resources in Cooperation with Foreign Enterprise", "Policies on the Utilization of Natural Gas", etc. will be revised to be more suitable for the new characteristics of various aspects in natural gas exploration, production, transportation, storage, distribution, and utilization. The conflicts between "Oil and Natural Gas Pipeline Protection Law" and other laws will be settled through judicial interpretation and other means.

Reinforce the industry regulation. China will establish a natural gas regulation system covering the whole industry chain and process to reinforce the governmental regulations on market access, trading behavior, monopoly, taxation, price and cost, quality, safety, environmental protection and other key aspects. It will accelerate the improvement of natural gas industry standardization system. More attention will be paid to information disclosure and social supervision, elaborating the bridge role of societal organizations and third parties on social supervision, and media's positive effect on environmental protection knowledge propaganda and disclosure of illegal activities, etc.

（五）完善支持天然气发展的政策体系

强化环境保护指标硬约束。加快散煤治理和工业燃料升级。以"三区十群"为重点，设定并逐步扩大"禁煤区"范围，加快城市、乡镇生活燃料以气代煤以及燃煤锅炉、排放不达标的燃油工业锅炉和窑炉的天然气替代。建立对各省（自治区、直辖市）环保措施的考核问责机制，将天然气替代煤炭纳入考核内容。各地能源监管部门对"禁煤区"内的煤炭生产、流通、使用实施严格监管。

完善产业政策体系。以"三区十群"工业燃料升级为主要切入点，制定实施更加严格的污染物排放标准，加大天然气替代煤炭力度。在内河和近海重点地区扩大船舶排放控制区范围，并将船舶控排区实施方案尽快提升至法规层面。加快碳排放立法工作，在工业燃料和发电领域中对燃煤、燃油及天然气采取同一标准安排碳排放配额，碳排放交易由目前的七个试点省市扩展到全国省市区，尽快建立全国统一碳排放交易市场。参照非水可再生能源发电配额制，研究制定燃煤火电机组天然气发电的配额制政策。优化加气站、加注站规划建站审批，鼓励更多的社会资本投资，支持 CNG 加气站扩建成 CNG/LNG 两用站，鼓励油气合建站、油气电合建站发展，鼓励建设岸基、水上 LNG 船舶加注站，加快相关标准规范制修订。清理规范天然气产业税费，推进费改税，对确应保留的合理收费，须尽快立法。

加强财税、投融资等政策支持。加大"以气代煤"央地两级财政补贴力度，向燃煤锅炉、窑炉改天然气企业提供低息贷

(5) Improving Policy System for Supporting Natural Gas Development

Reinforce the hard constraints on environment protection. Bulk coal control and industrial fuel update will be accelerated. Focusing on "Three-district Ten-group", China will set and gradually expand the "Coal-free Zone", to speed up the replacement with natural gas in urban and rural living fuel, coal-fired boiler, oil-fired industrial boilers and furnaces. In the assessment accountability mechanisms for environmental protection measures of every province (autonomous regions and municipalities), "Coal-to-Gas" will be included in the assessment content. Local energy regulatory authorities implement strict regulation on coal production, circulation and use in "Coal-free Zone"

Improve the industrial policy system. Take the industrial fuel upgrade in "Three-district Ten-group" as the main entry point, more stringent emission standards will be developed and implemented, increasing the intensity of "Coal-to-Gas". Vessel emission control areas will be expanded in key areas of inland waters and coastal waters. The vessel emission control program will be updated to regulatory level as soon as possible. The legislation of carbon emission will be accelerated. The same carbon emission quota will be adopted for coal, oil and natural gas in industrial fuel and power generation fields. The carbon emissions trading will be expanded from the current seven pilot provincial urban areas to the provincial urban areas nation-widely, to establish as soon as possible a unified nation-wide carbon emission trading system. Referring to the power generation quota system for non-hydropower renewable energy, the quota policy of natural gas power generation using coal-fired power units will be studied and established. The approval process of gas stations and filling stations will be optimized, encouraging more social capital investments to support the expansion of CNG station to CNG/LNG dual station. Oil and gas station, oil-gas-electricity station, land-based and waterborne LNG vessel filling stations will be encouraged with accelerated relevant standards and regulations development and revision. China will clean up and regulate natural gas industry taxes and fees, promoting "Fee-to-Tax". The reasonable fees which should be retained will be legislated as soon as possible.

Strengthen the taxation, investment and financing policy support. The financial subsidies on "Coal-to-Gas" from the central and local governments

款和土地收益返还等政策。参照垃圾和生物质电厂增值税退税政策，对天然气发电用户给予相应的增值税减免。参照新能源汽车支持政策，给予天然气汽车购置补贴、燃料补贴等补贴政策，取消向车用气收取调节基金，燃气公交车与燃油公交车享受相同的补贴政策。对以旧换新船舶和改造单燃料 LNG 船舶设立专项补贴，对新增 LNG 船舶延续船型标准化资金补贴办法。对天然气基础设施企业给予税收政策扶持，在 2016—2025 年实行增值税实际税负超 3% 即征即退。支持符合条件的天然气基础设施企业发行企业债券融资，支持储气设施建设项目发行项目收益债券；支持地方政府投融资平台公司，通过发行企业债券建设天然气基础设施；上述企业债券融资均不受年度发债规模指标限制。

加大科技创新。 尽快推进天然气利用装备（包括重型燃气轮机、适合分布式供能的兆瓦级微小燃气轮机、车用第五代高压直喷发动机、大型 LNG 船用单燃料发动机等）科技攻关及国产化。探索研发集装箱方式运输 LNG 的技术和装备，增强 LNG 运输的灵活性。鼓励并引导 LNG 整车企业加大对电控、发动机、气瓶和蒸发气体回收等方面技术的研发力度。

will be increased. Enterprises who transfer coal-fired boilers and furnaces to natural gas will obtain low interest loans and return of land revenue. Based on the value-added tax rebate policy for the garbage and biomass power plants, natural gas power plants will be provided with the corresponding value-added tax relief. According to the support policy for new energy vehicles, natural gas vehicle purchase and fuel subsides will be implemented, the regulating fund charged for providing gas to vehicles will be canceled, and both the natural gas buses and fuel buses will have the same subsidy policy. Special subsidies will be set up for old vessel trade-ins and single fuel LNG vessel rebuilt. For new LNG vessels, the standardized subsidy method will be continued. Taxation policy support will be provided to natural gas infrastructure enterprises. In 2016—2025, if the actual tax burden of value-added tax is over 3%, such tax will be refunded. Qualified natural gas infrastructure companies will be supported to issue corporate bond financing and gas storage facilities construction projects will be supported to issue project income bonds. Local governmental investment and financing platform companies will be encouraged to construct natural gas infrastructure through the issuance of corporate bonds. The above corporate bond financings are not subject to the annual debt issuance quota.

Speedup scientific development and technological innovation. The technological development and localization of natural gas utilization equipment will be advanced as soon as possible, including heavy duty gas turbine, MW class micro gas turbine suitable for distributed energy supply, the fifth generation high pressure direct injection engine for vehicle, large LNG marine single fuel engine, etc. The technology and equipment for transporting the LNG using container will be explored and developed, in order to enhance the flexibility of LNG transport. LNG vehicle enterprises will be encouraged and guided to develop the technology on the electronic control, engine, LNG cylinder and boil-off gas recycle to improve the efficiency of natural gas vehicles.

结束语

从中国实际出发，坚持天然气快速发展并与可再生能源融合发展是中国能源转型的必然选择。2030年是中国全面建成小康社会后的第一个十年，也是实现"两个一百年"奋斗目标为第二个百年奠定基础的关键时期。尽快提升天然气在一次能源结构中的比重，把天然气发展成为中国的主体能源，有利于优化和调整能源结构，建成天然气与可再生能源、新能源以及石油和煤炭多能互补的现代能源体系，为中国经济实力和综合国力再上新台阶提供充足的能源保障；有利于加快能源技术创新和产业升级，加快推进生态文明建设，显著增强中国应对世界气候变化能力，构建发挥中国积极作用的新型世界能源治理体系。

《中国天然气发展报告》今后将每年发布一次，旨在搭建一个持续推进中国能源大转型与探索天然气产业健康、快速发展的交流沟通平台。在此，我们诚挚地感谢各相关部门、研究机构、高等院校、行业学会、企业、国际机构以及众多专家的大力支持和帮助。

Concluding Remarks

For China to modernize through green growth, adhering to the rapid development of natural gas and integrating with renewable energy development is the inevitable choice of China's energy transformation. The decade leading to 2030 is China's first decade after fully building a well-off society in an all-round way by 2020, and is also a critical period to lay down the foundation for achieving the second of the "Two Centenary Goals". Increasing the proportion of natural gas in the primary energy structure as soon as possible, and developing natural gas to be China's main energy source are conducive to optimizing and adjusting the energy structure, building a complementary modern energy system comprised of natural gas, renewable energy, new energy, oil and coal, providing adequate energy security for the growth of China's economy and comprehensive national strength. This is also conducive to accelerating energy technology innovation and industrial upgrading, speeding up the construction of ecological civilization, and significantly enhancing China's ability to cope with climate change, as well as building a positive role of China in the new world energy governance system.

"China Natural Gas Development Report" will be issued annually from now on, aiming to build a communication platform that continuously promotes the grand transformation of China energy, and explore the healthy and rapid development of its natural gas industry.

图书在版编目（CIP）数据

中国天然气发展报告. 2016/ 国家能源局石油天然气司，国务院发展研究中心资源与环境政策研究所，国土资源部油气资源战略研究中心编.
北京：石油工业出版社，2016.12

ISBN 978-7-5183-1677-9

Ⅰ. 中…
Ⅱ. ①国…
②国…
③国…
Ⅲ. ①天然气工业 – 研究报告 – 中国 –2016
Ⅳ. ①F426.22
中国版本图书馆 CIP 数据核字（2016）第 281888 号

出版发行：石油工业出版社
（北京安定门外安华里2区1号　100011）
网　　址：www.petropub.com
编辑部：（010）64523543　图书营销中心：（010）64523633
经　　销：全国新华书店
印　　刷：北京中石油彩色印刷有限责任公司

2016年12月第1版　2016年12月第1次印刷
787×1092毫米　开本：1/16　印张：3.5
字数：90千字

定价：48.00元
（如出现印装质量问题，我社图书营销中心负责调换）
版权所有，翻印必究